NATURE'S R  G

RIDDLES

To Oliver,
"Happy Rhyming!"
Michael J. Larson ☺

WRITTEN BY

MICHAEL J. LARSON

ILLUSTRATED BY

JANINE RINGDAHL SCHMIDT

Nature's Rhyming Riddles

Printed in the United States of America.

ISBN   978-1-951961-40-4   (Hardback)
ISBN   978-1-951961-38-1   (Paperback)
ISBN   978-1-951961-39-8   (Digital)

Pen House books may be ordered through booksellers or by contacting:

Pen House LLC
30 N Gould St. Suite 4752
Sheridan, WY 82801
1 307-212-5979 | info@penhousellc.com
www.penhousellc.com

Hints we will give you in these lines that rhyme,

About creatures with hair, scales or a covering of
   slime.

As you read the hints found on each page,

Don't get frustrated or filled up with rage.

Instead listen to the rhyming hints with care,

And before long the mystery creature's name you will
   share!

This animal spends time in the hollow of trees,
At night travels our highways and in our headlights
  it flees.
It roams the farm fields searching for snacks,
Never far from the water's edge where often we
  see its tracks.

When it's hungry it will dine on a frog or a fish,

The dirty ground serves as the table and there is no need for a dish.

For dessert it may devour berries, plums, nuts or seeds,

Or travel to a sweet corn patch and eat all it needs!

Its footprint contains five toes and resembles our hand,

We see its impression in pond mud and in damp sand.

If we followed the footprints to see where they go,

They would travel in circles and confuse us I know!

We wear rings on our fingers and this is a fact,

If this animal wore rings on its tail how would you react?

Well, it does have rings on its tail and a mask on its face,

Sounds like it's been snooping around a Halloween costume place!

JRS

Well these are the hints and now what do you say,
Can you guess what this animal is right away?
Right away would certainly not be too soon,
Especially if you guessed a furry raccoon!

When you were small and your Mom hollered,
"Lunch",
How would you like eating earthworms, one or a
bunch?
As this animal grew older its diet became grander,
Along with earthworms it ate frogs, toads, fish and
even a salamander!

Wanting to capture one to put in a zoo,

I would search the environment for a possible clue.

If it had been there we would know by its tracks,

But wait, that is impossible, because legs are something it lacks!

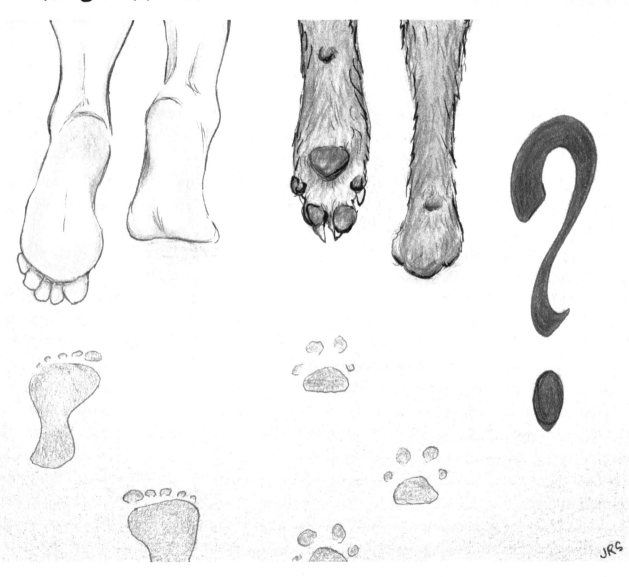

If it is cornered and suffering from fright,
Put out your hand and it will give you a 'not serious'
bite.
Grab it and hold it while its fear still rages,
It will release a fluid causing your hands to stink
for ages!

This animal has skin that can only stretch so far,

And as the animal grows something happens bizarre!

The scaly skin loosens first at the head,

In a short period of time its skin has been shed.

Do you know this animal that has been just described?

If so, would you tell us without being bribed?

It has startled us on lawns, gardens and even next
   to a lake,

It is the harmless and often seen garter snake!

This animal drifts for hours high in the sky,
Using thermal currents to rise thousands of feet,
we wonder why?
They flap and glide to maintain their great view,
And then suddenly descend to earth as if on cue.

In the shallows of lakes, sloughs, rivers and streams,
This animal goes in search of fish for hours it seems.
Sometimes they join together and swim in a line,
They chase fish into the shallows and upon them
they dine.

Eggs are laid in nests in depressed ground or low trees,

For thirty days Mom and Pop incubate the eggs without one please!

When the little babies hatch both naked and blind,

They are fed food from their parents' bills, the digested kind!

In the animal kingdom this creature might be considered a 'geek',
Largely because of its enormous and odd-shaped beak.
The upper part is flattened, bright orange and firm,
The lower half is designed to net fish as they flop and they squirm.

And now do you know of what animal we speak?

We can be sure it's a bird since it contains a beak.

And the beak is large with the bottom half forming
a pouch,

If you guessed a White Pelican I would say you're
no slouch!

Nocturnal, nocturnal a night creature is he,
If you're driving at night in your head lights he'll be.
Drive carefully, steer well and do not run him down,
Because if you do you'll not be popular in town!

When you discover holes dug in the grass under
    your shrubs,
Likely the holes were dug by this animal looking for
    grubs.
Also it eats eggs, berries, insects and mice,
And a road-killed pheasant would also be nice.

Suppose this animal was an actor starring on the big screen,

When asked to make a 'black and white' movie would it stomp and make a scene?

Of course not, it would be polite and not play the tantrum game,

Whether it was in 'black and white' or Technicolor it would always look the same.

This animal protects itself in an unusual manner,
Facing its enemy, stamping front paws and raising
   its tail like

                              a bushy banner.

If the enemy is not frightened nor does it back away,
The threatened animal turns its back and releases
   a foul

                              smelling spray!

Do you know, do you know of what creature we speak?

It must be clear when you hear of its spray that does reek!

There is no quicker way to get yourself into a funk,

Then to be downwind from the spray of a big Striped Skunk!

This animal is cold-blooded and is the temperature
of the air,

On cool days check sunny slopes and you'll always
find some there.

Or in the early evening after the sun has set,

Finding them on warm tar roads is a very good bet.

In their mouth the tongue is not fastened in back,
But placed up front where it can mount an attack.
Like a sticky rubber band it flails and wraps,
In the blink of an eye an insect it entraps!

JRS

They are cute little babies when they are small,
But they resemble their parents not at all.
Eggs laid in water develop and hatch,
Producing tiny offspring that children love to catch!

Large back legs allow this animal to make an awe-
    some jump,
Trying to catch one, however, can turn you into a
    grump!
The back legs, they say, are tasty when fried just so,
If you eat its back legs, however, it loses its 'get up
    and go'!

So do you know what animal is cold blooded and
   hops?
And with a long, sticky tongue for insects it shops?
Take a walk to a pond, a lake or a bog,
And I guarantee you'll discover a green Leopard
   Frog!

The mysteries are over, the guesswork is done,
Learning about animals, I think, is quite fun.

A raccoon may rattle your garbage can at night,
While a slithering garter snake may give you a fright.

A line of swimming White Pelicans may demonstrate
    how to fish,
And a Striped Skunk will teach you how to say "ish"!

A green Leopard Frog may hop on your toe,
And after reading this book, think how your knowl-
    edge will grow!

About the author

Michael J. Larson's first seven books have been written in the prose form. Over the years he has produced a lot of rhymes in the form of birthday greetings, graduation cards and Facebook posts however this is his first attempt at producing a published work in rhymes. The author spent forty-two years educating students about God's beautiful world as a biology teacher. He and his wife, Kathie, have three children and eight grandchildren. They live on a small acreage in western Minnesota, where the author blogs, gardens, plays golf, reads and enjoys the peace and quiet of the outdoors. He can be contacted by email at mklarson@frontiernet.net.

About the Artist

Janine Schmidt grew up in Wheaton, Minnesota, and earned her bachelor of fine arts degree from the Minneapolis College of Art and Design in 1989. She moved back to Wheaton, where she married Alan Schmidt. They have three children, Hannah, Nora and Nelson. Janine does a variety of different kinds of artwork but her favorite is illustrating children's books, especially for Mike Larson, her former biology teacher at Wheaton High School.

Book Dedication

I must dedicate this book to grandchildren so grand,
Who have enriched our lives more than they can understand.

First are the boys, Tristin, Logan and Bryce,
Followed by the girls, Brooke, Bree and Selena, how nice!

But stop, wait, we're not yet done,
We must not forget Caylin and Miah to round out the fun!

Grandpa Mike

CPSIA information can be obtained
at www.ICGtesting.com
Printed in the USA
BVHW020844260720
584559BV00004B/14